SBB

SWASTICK BOOK BOX
MASON OF WINNERS

Numbers
WRITING BOOK
1 to 20

Awesome Numbers Writing Practice Book for Kids

By: **Preeti Garg**

Follow the patterns with your pencil.

Date : ....

Teacher's Signature : ....

Follow the patterns with your pencil.

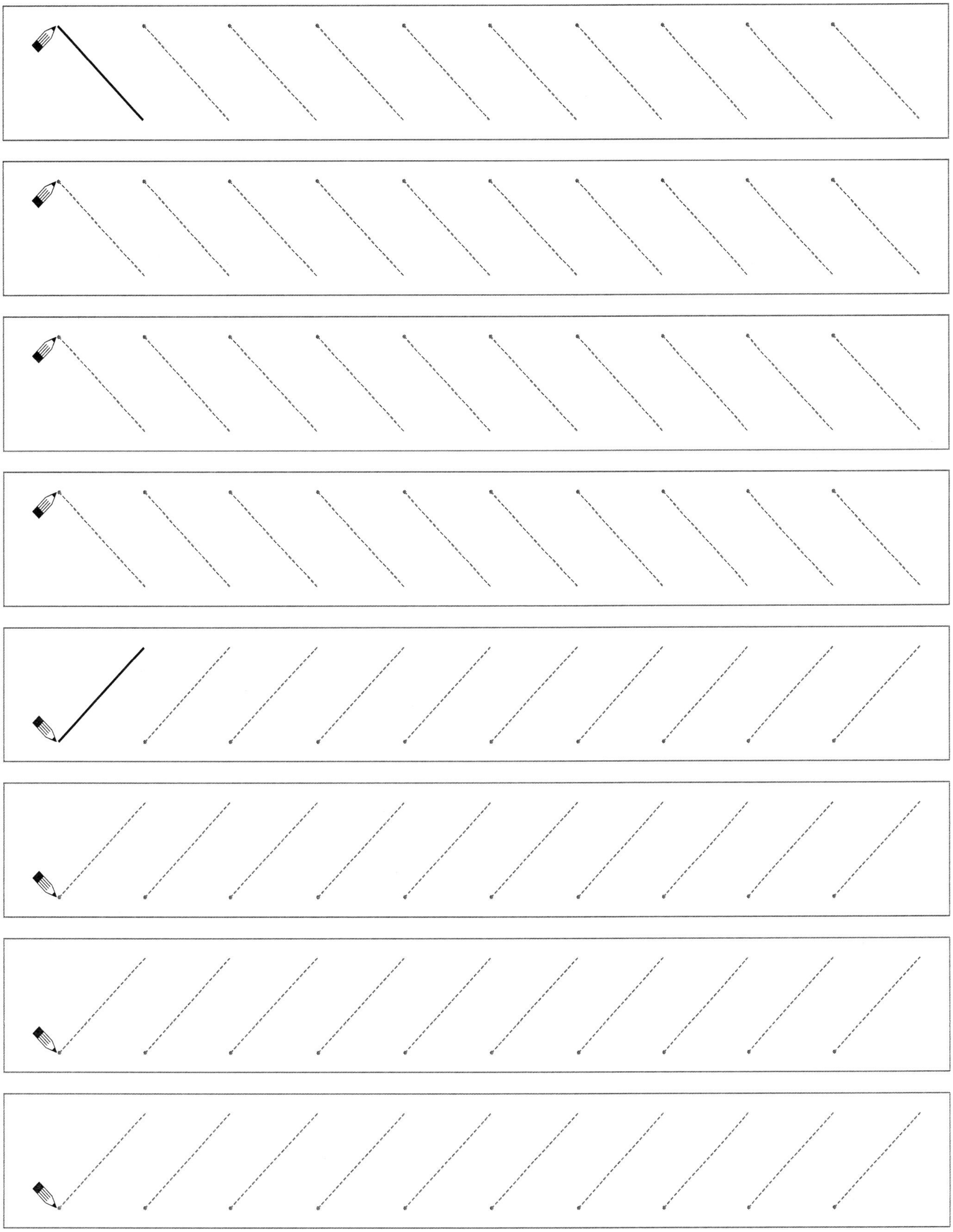

Date : ....

Teacher's Signature : ....

Follow the patterns with your pencil.

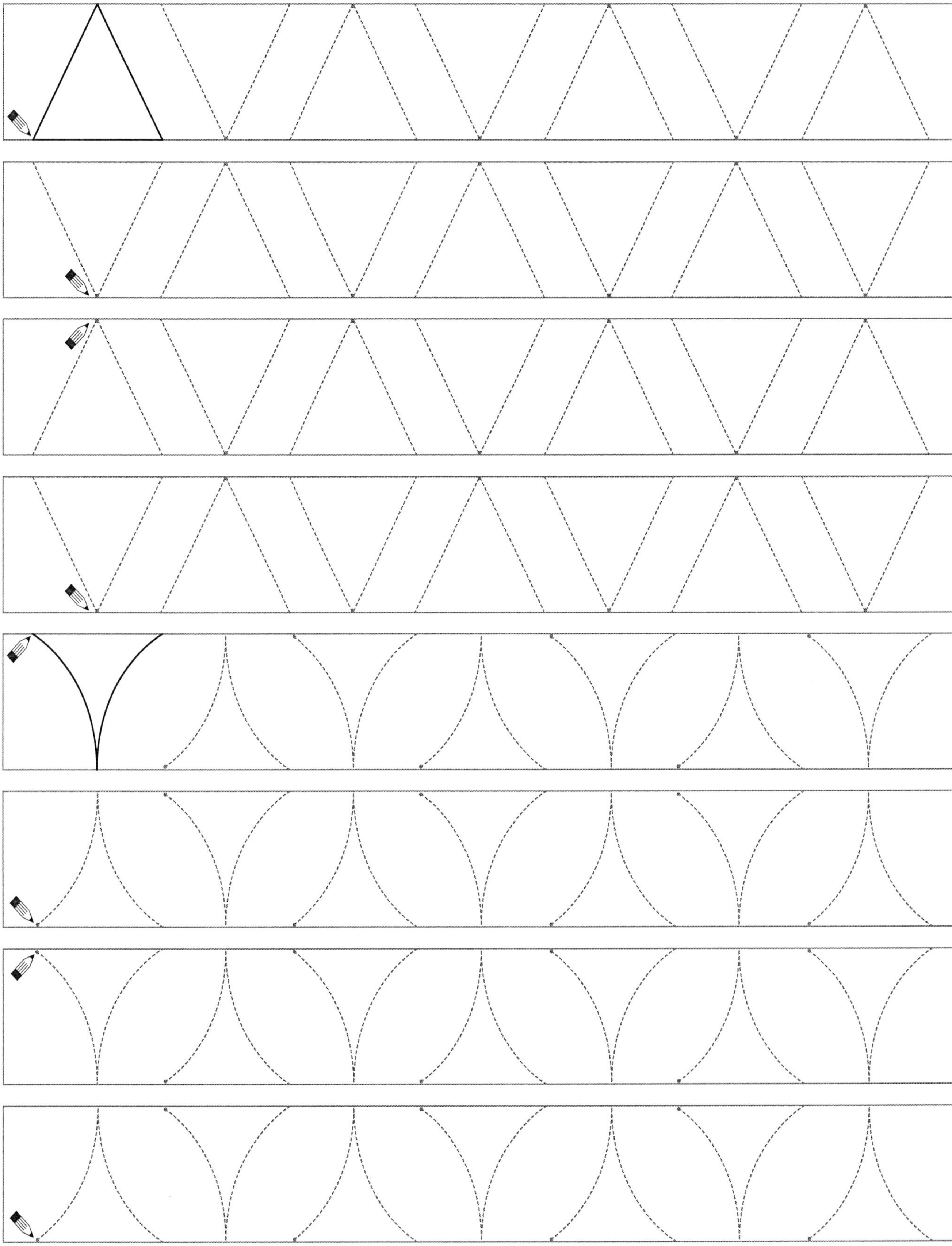

Date : ....

Teacher's Signature : ....

Follow the patterns with your pencil.

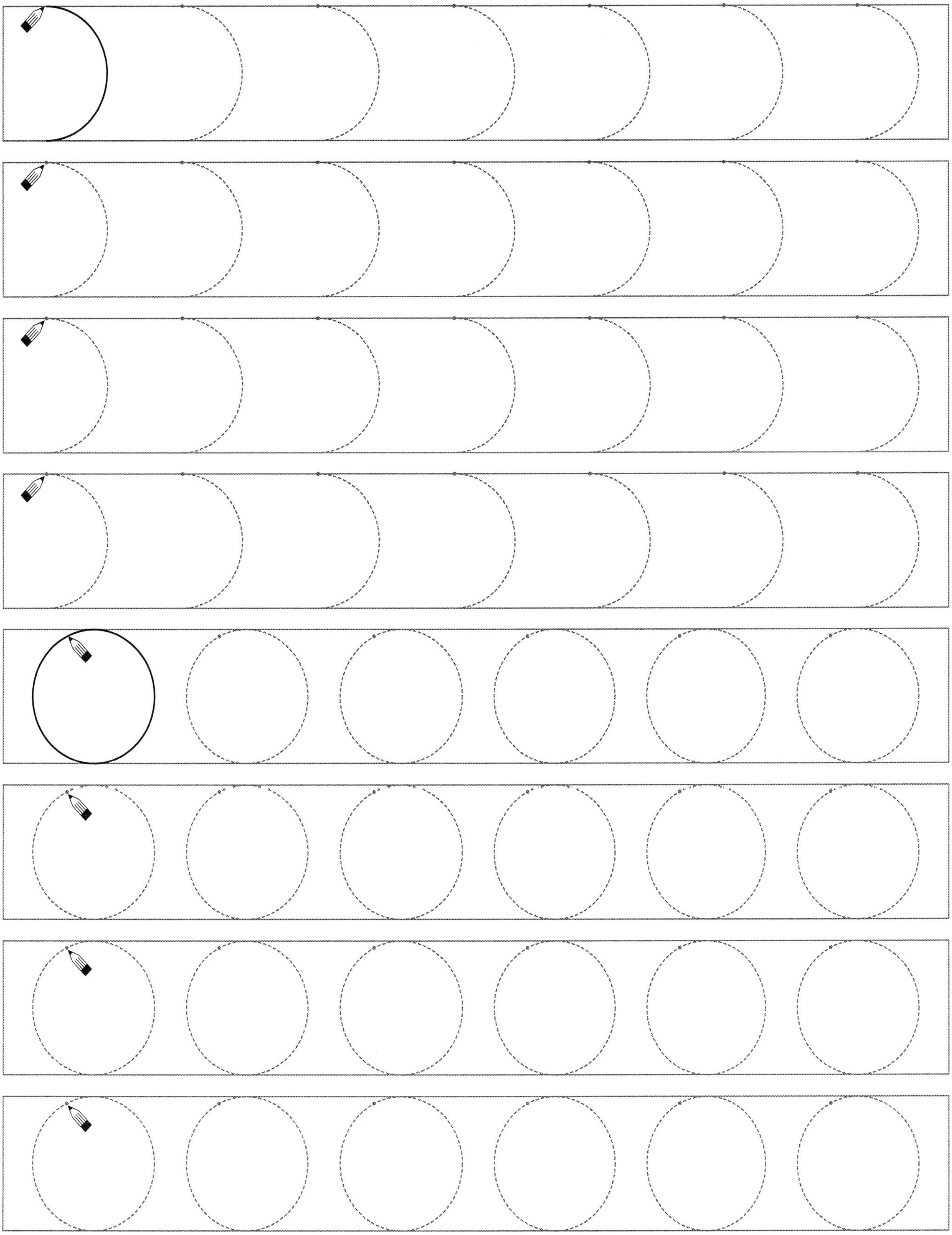

Date : ....

Teacher's Signature : ....

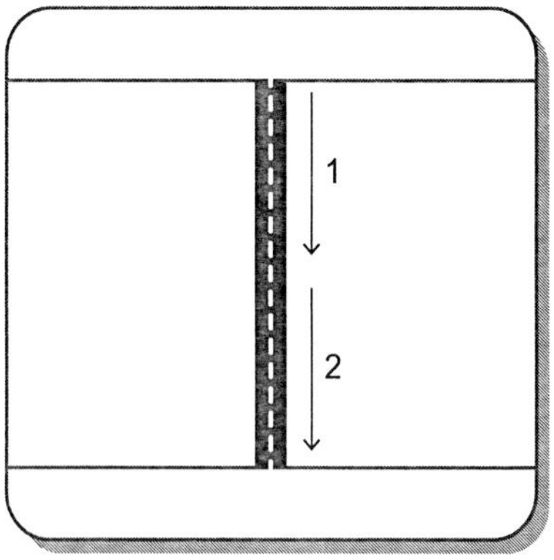

One

One Ice Cream

Date : ....

Teacher's Signature : ....

Two

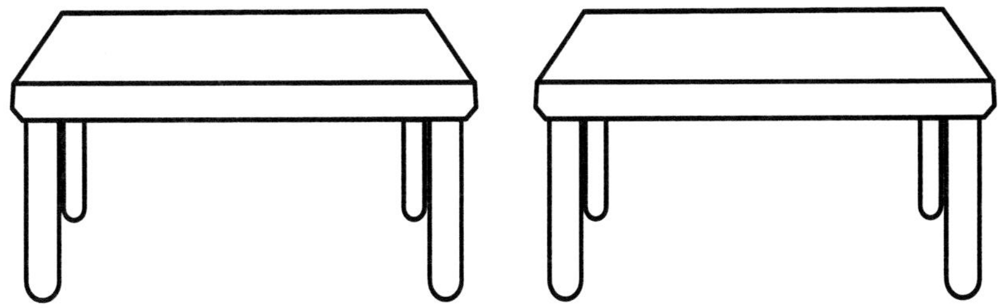

Two Tables

2

Three

Three Monkeys

3

Date : ....

Teacher's Signature : ....

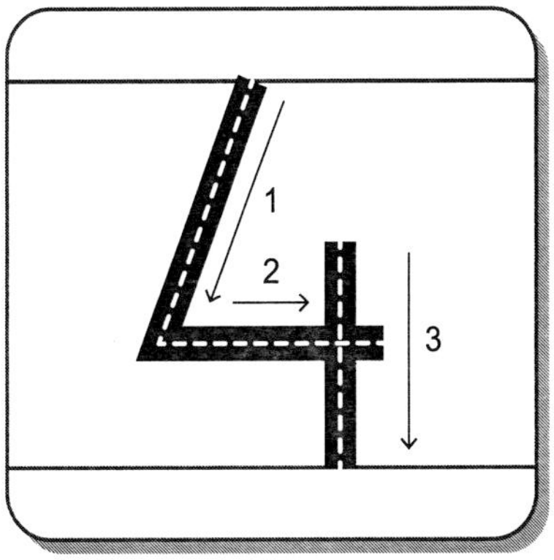

Four

Four Fans

Date : ....

Teacher's Signature : ....

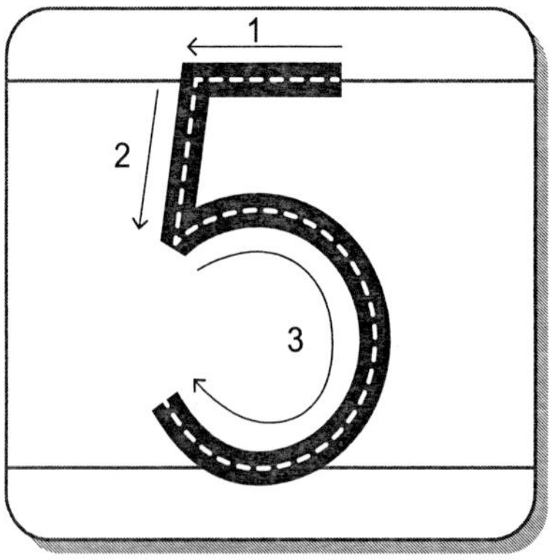

Five

Five Fishes

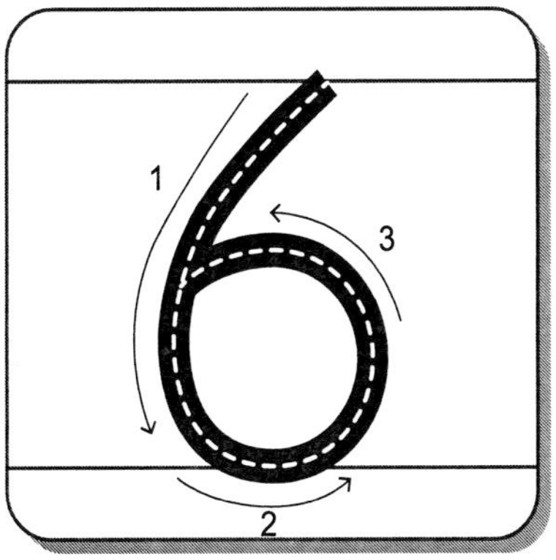

Six

Six Stars

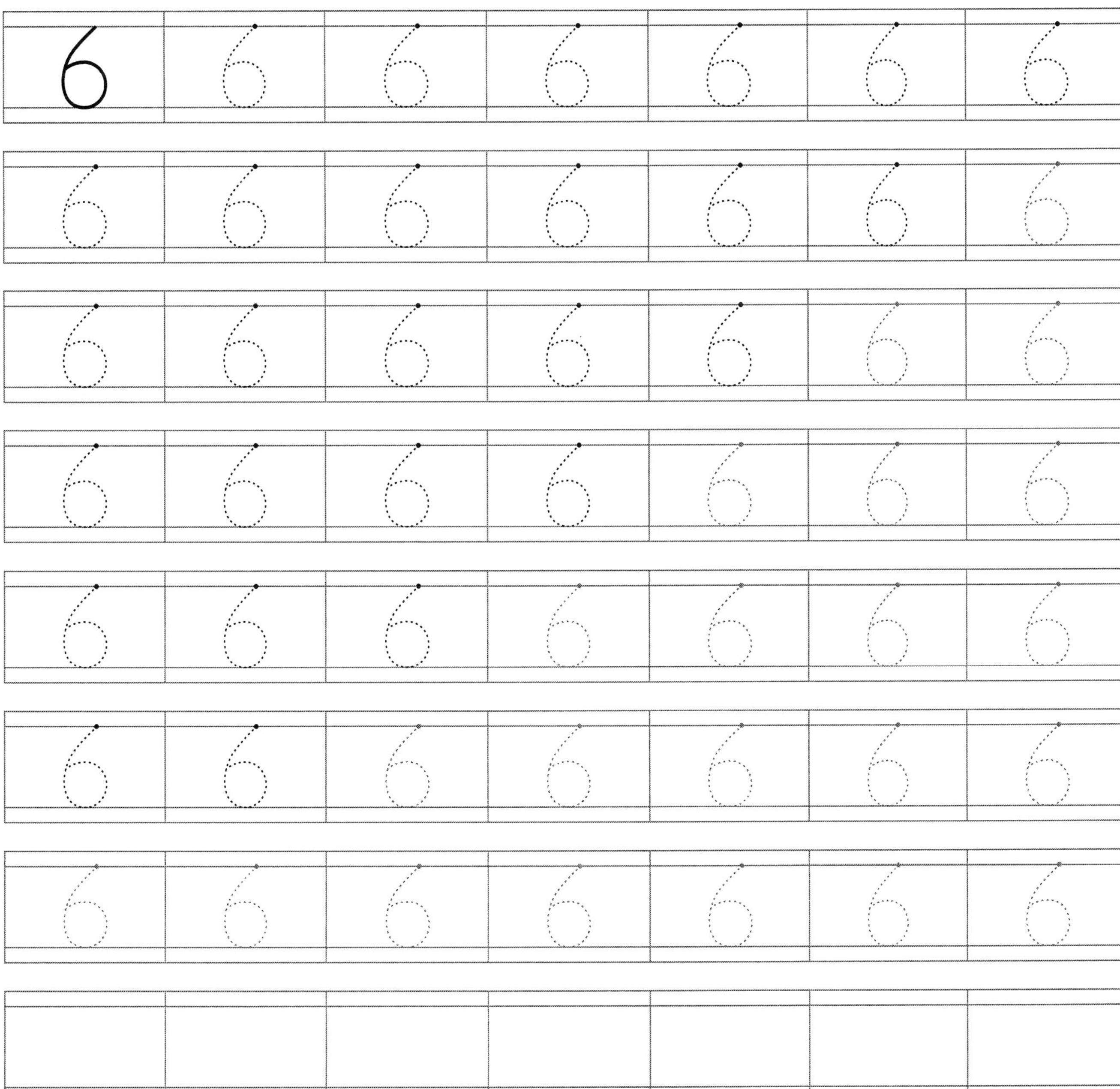

Date : ....

Teacher's Signature : ....

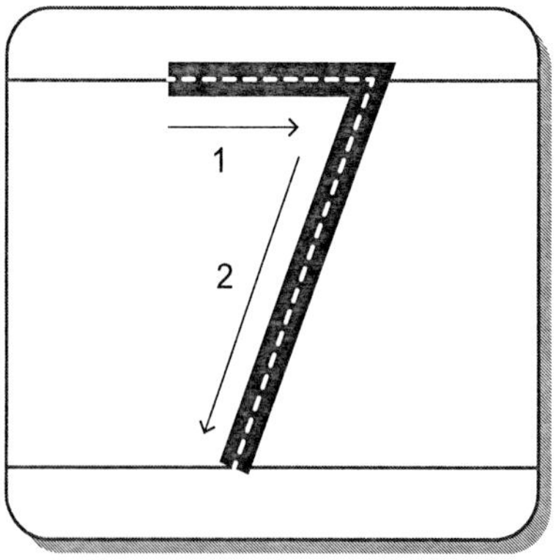

Seven

Seven Strawberries

Date : ....

Teacher's Signature : ....

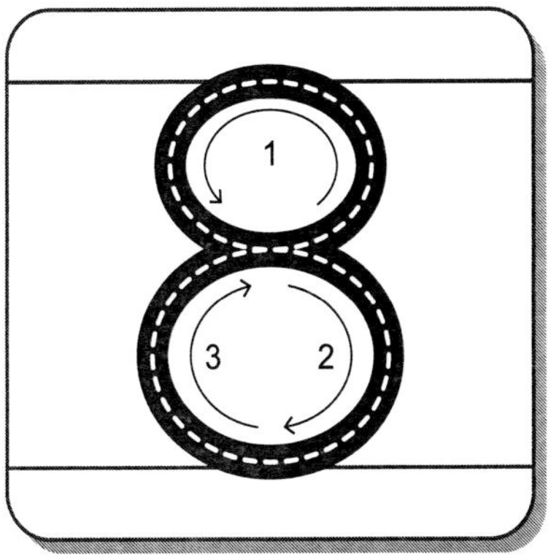

Eight

Eight Elephants

8

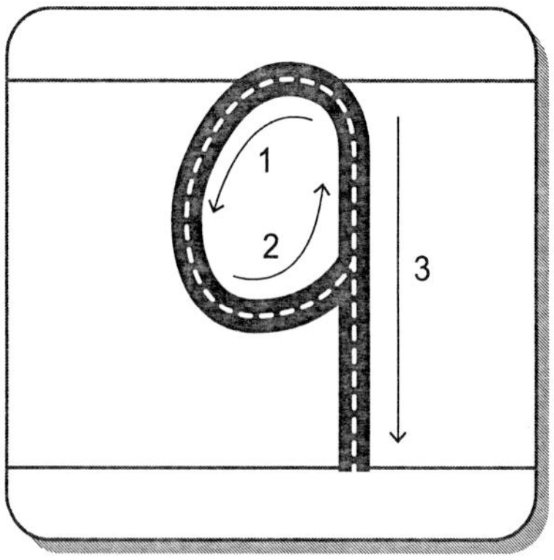

Nine

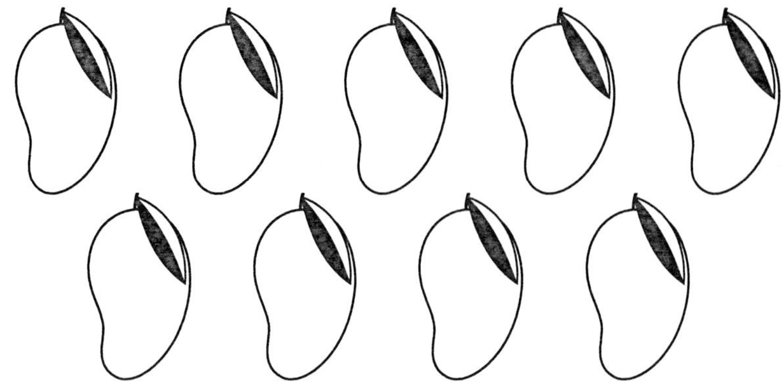

Nine Mangoes

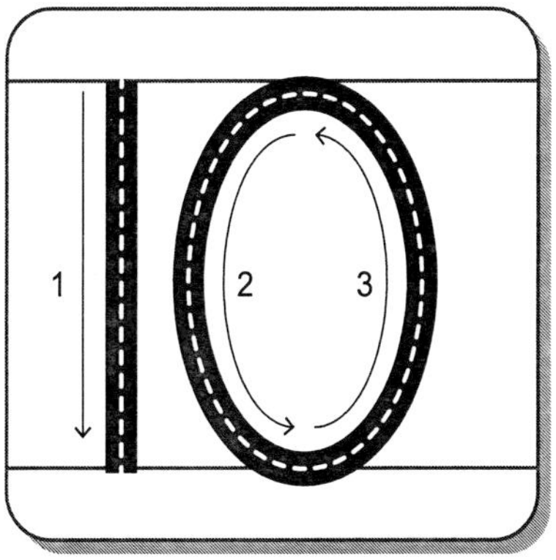

Ten

Ten Lamps

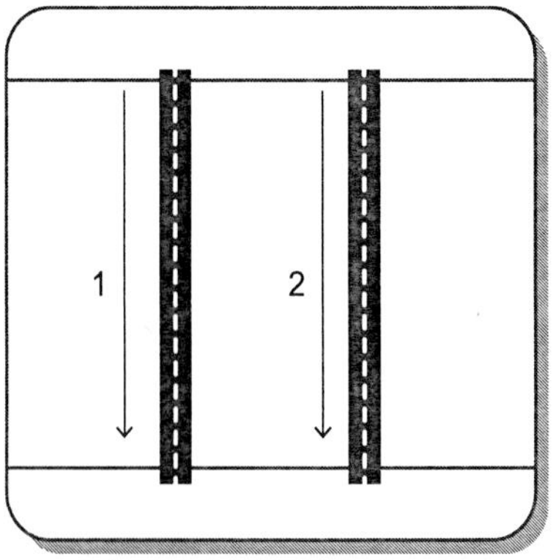

Eleven

Eleven Apples

Date : ....

Teacher's Signature : ....

Twelve

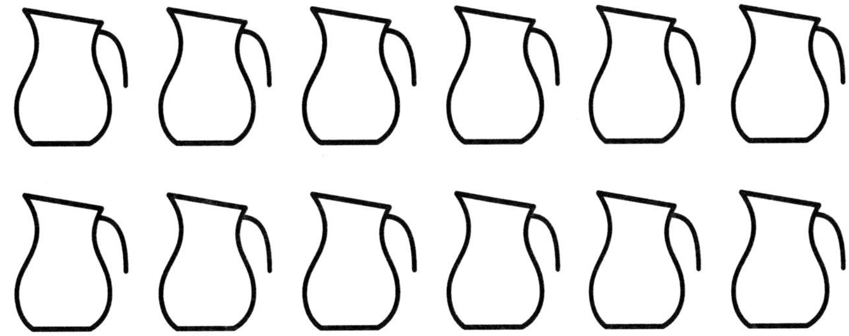

Twelve Jugs

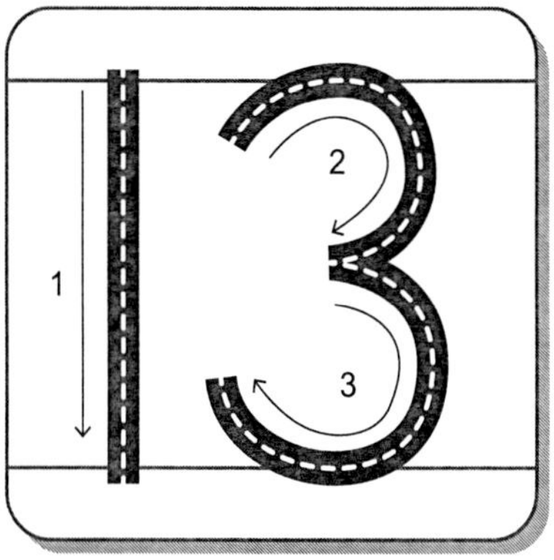

Thirteen

Thirteen Shoes

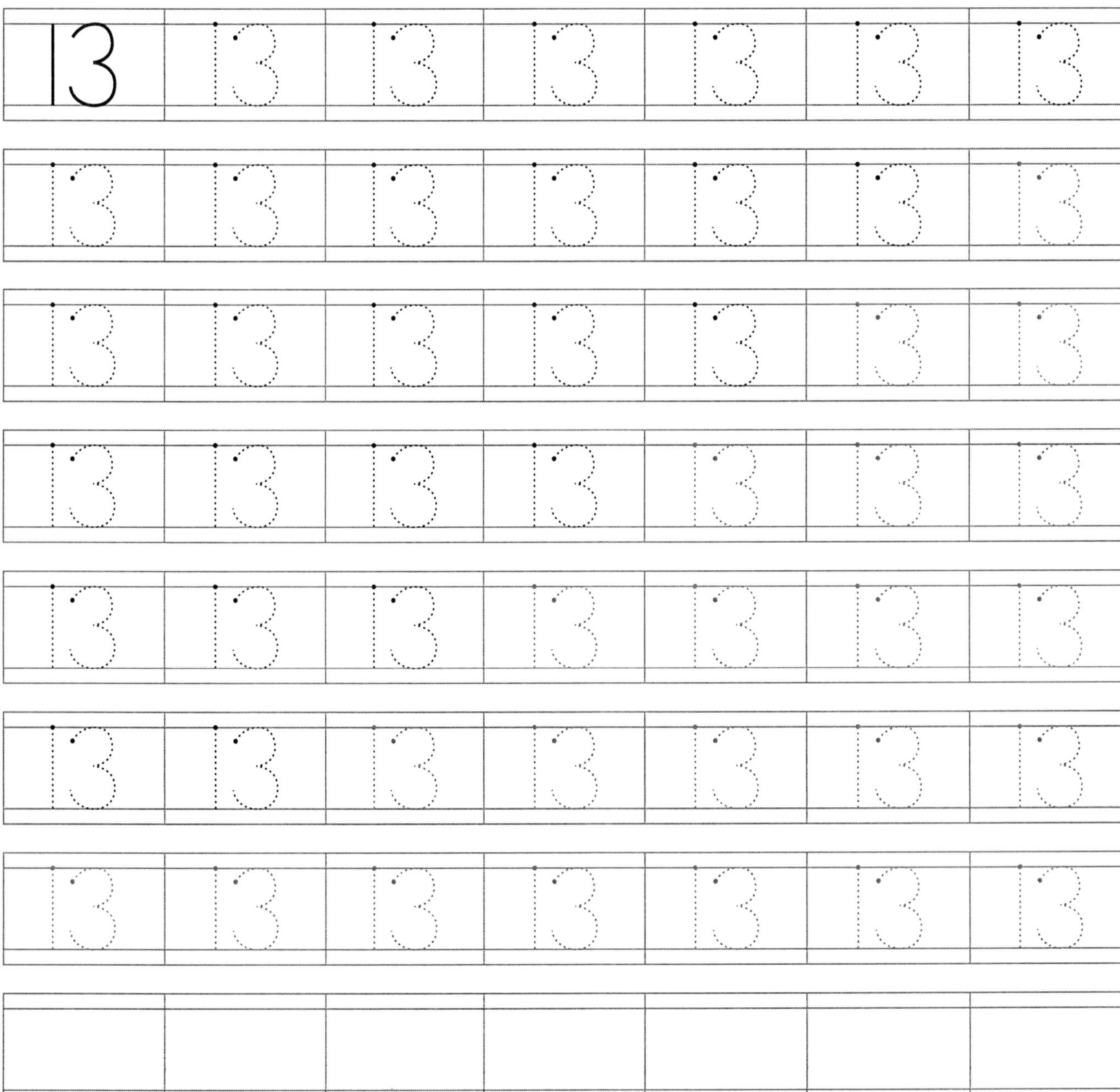

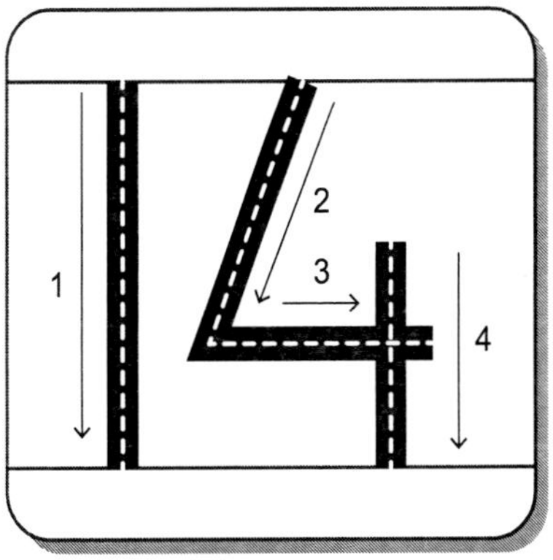

Fourteen

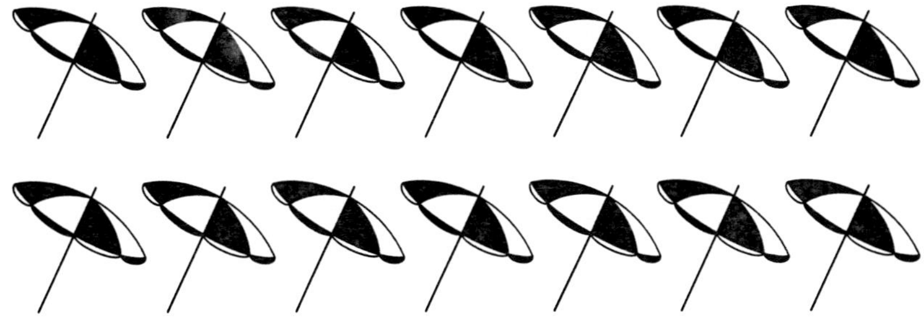

Fourteen Umbrellas

14

Date : ....

Teacher's Signature : ....

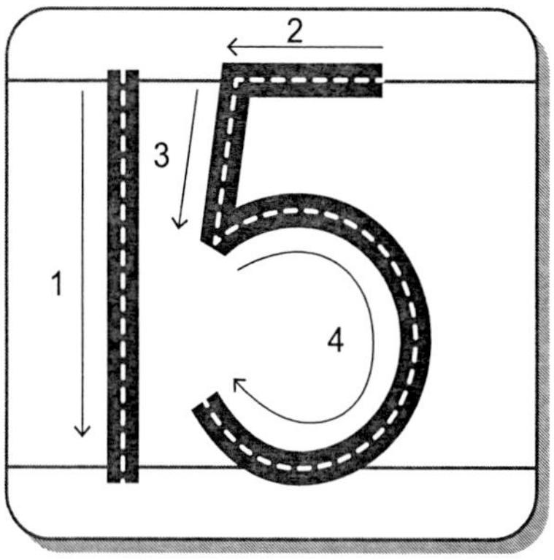

Fifteen

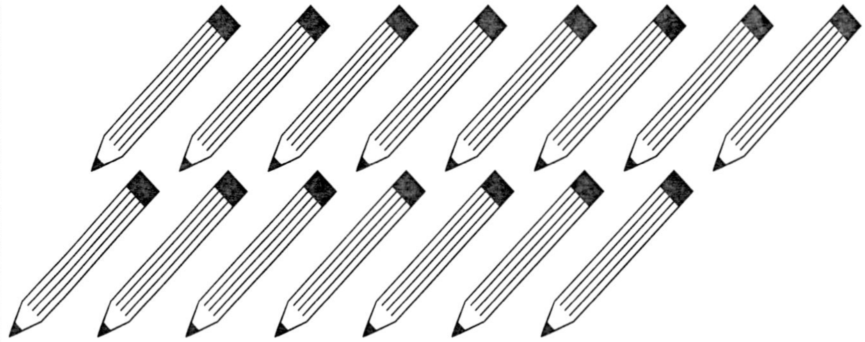

Fifteen Pencils

Date : ....

Teacher's Signature : ....

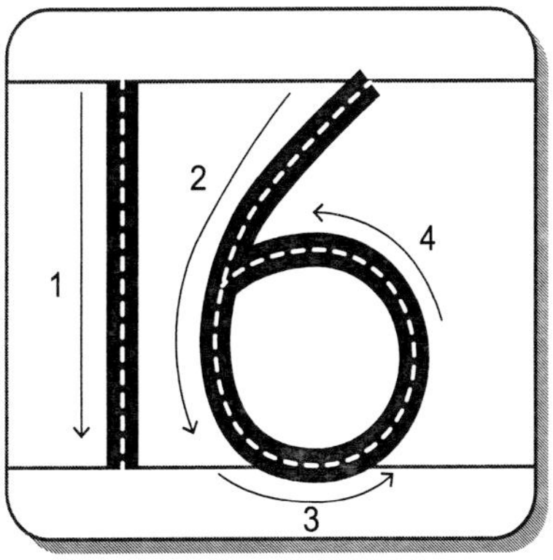

Sixteen

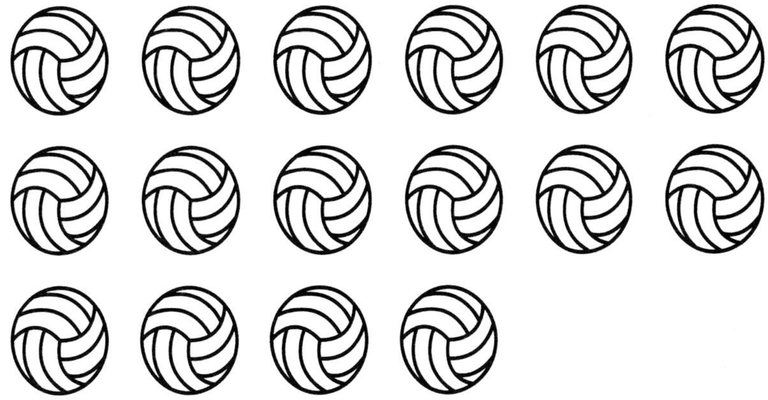

Sixteen Balls

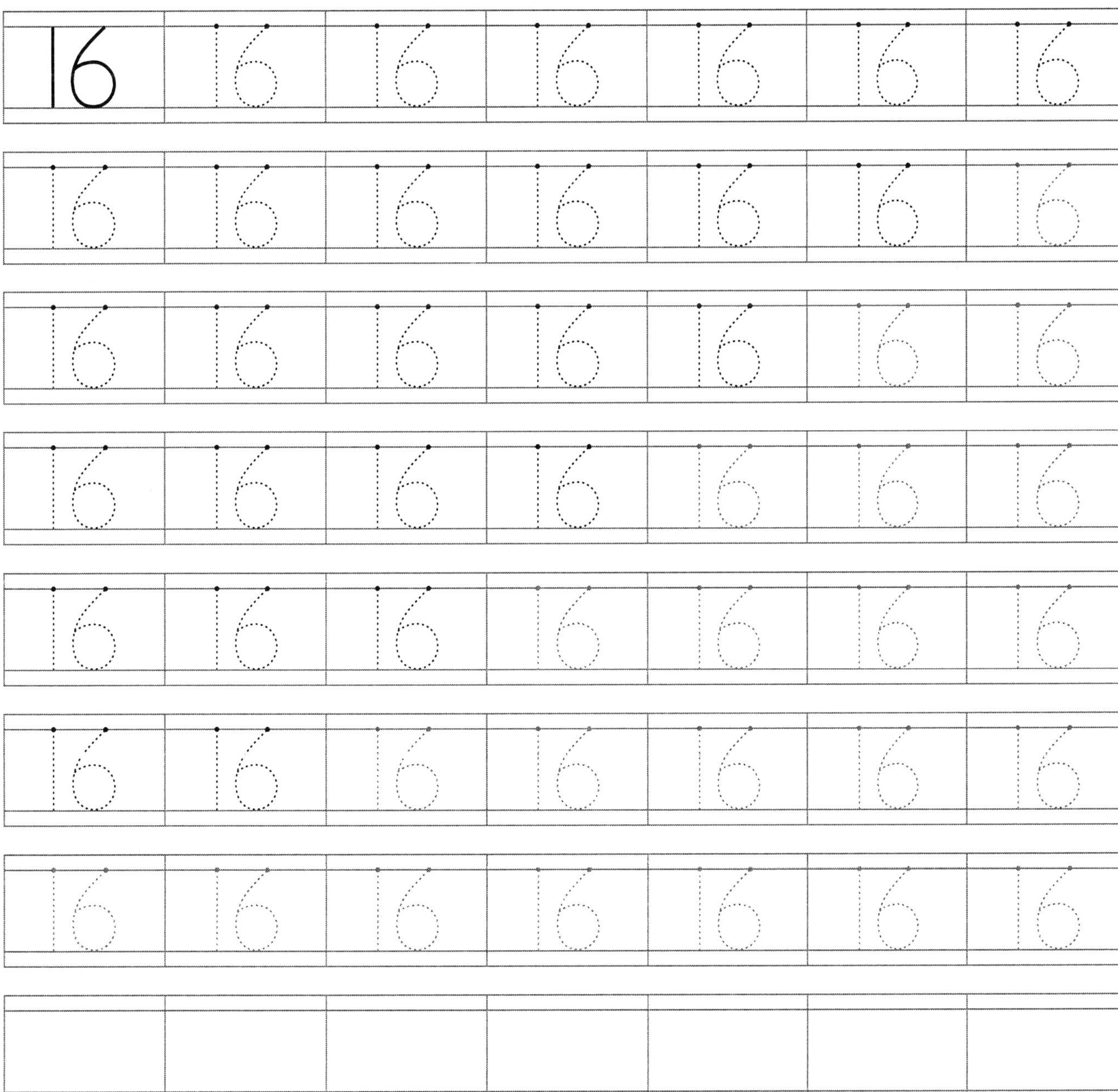

Date : ....

Teacher's Signature : ....

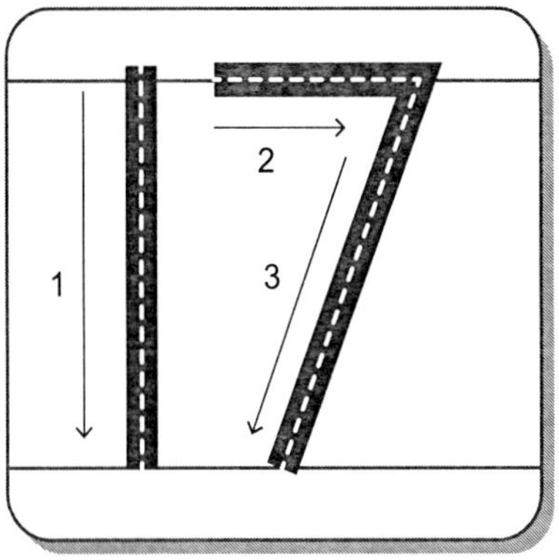

Seventeen

Seventeen Flowers

Date : ....

Teacher's Signature : ....

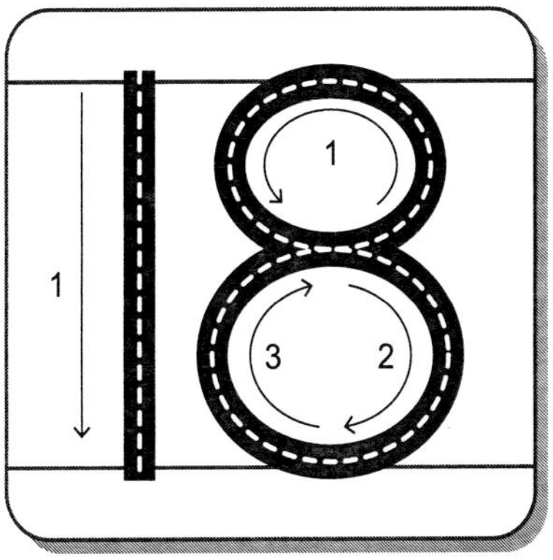

Eighteen

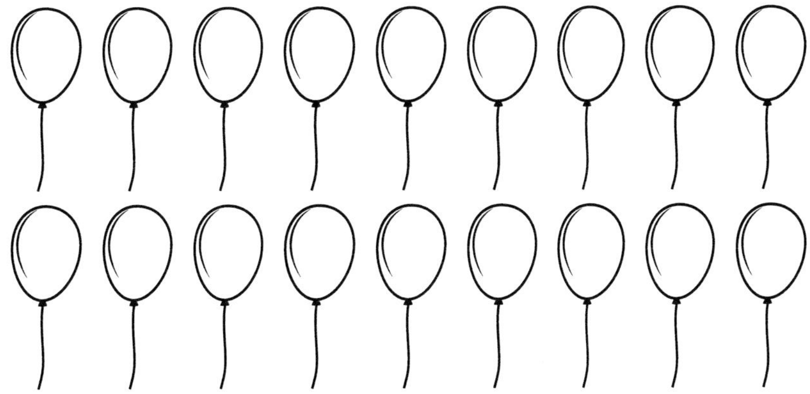

Eighteen Balloons

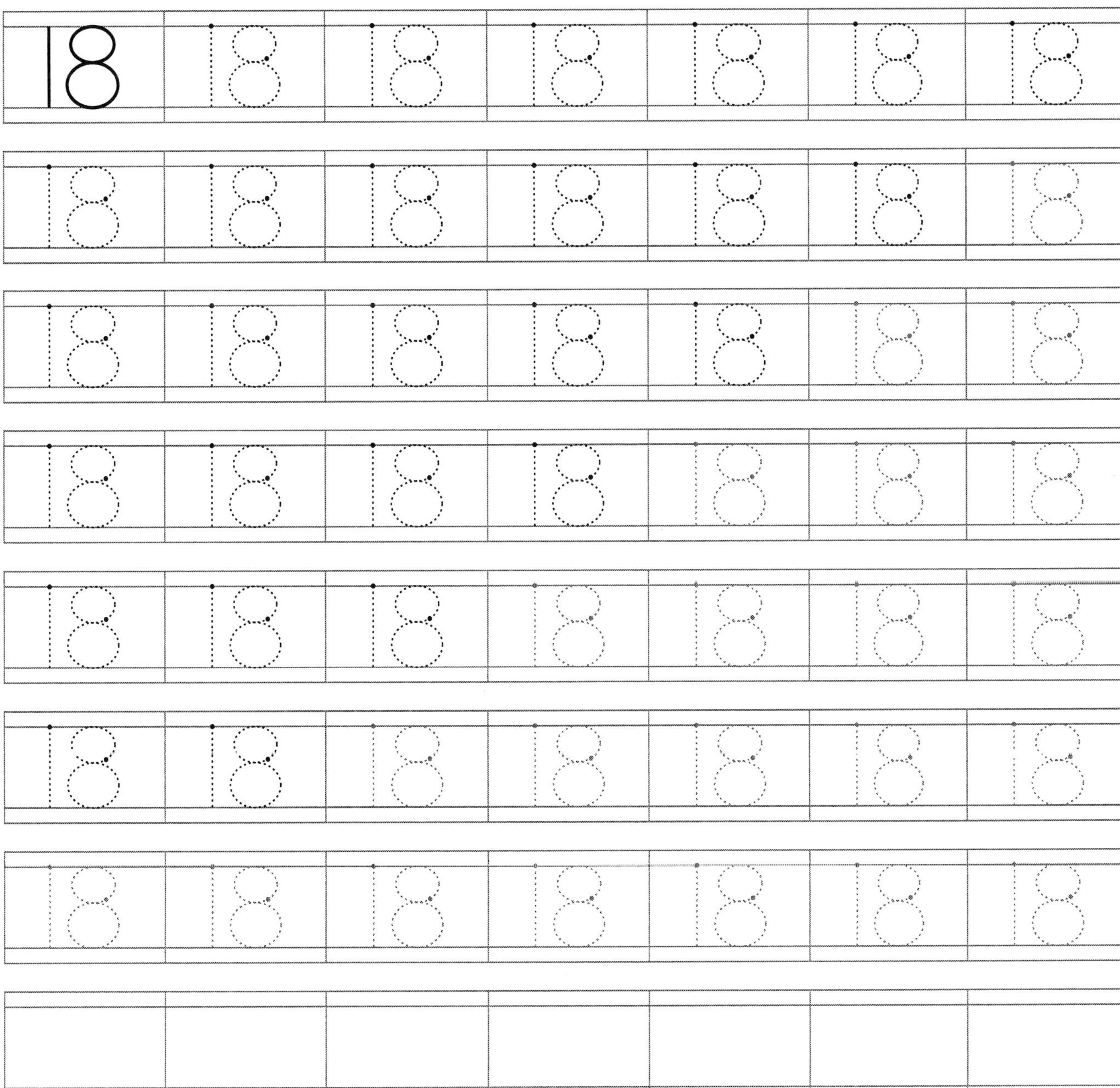

Date : ....

Teacher's Signature : ....

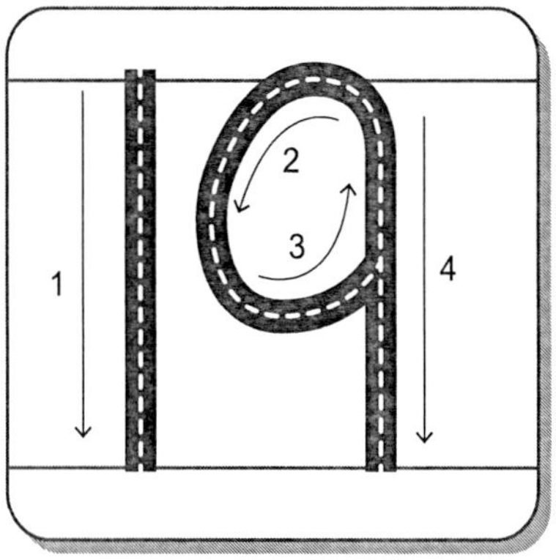

Nineteen

Nineteen Honey Bees

19

Twenty

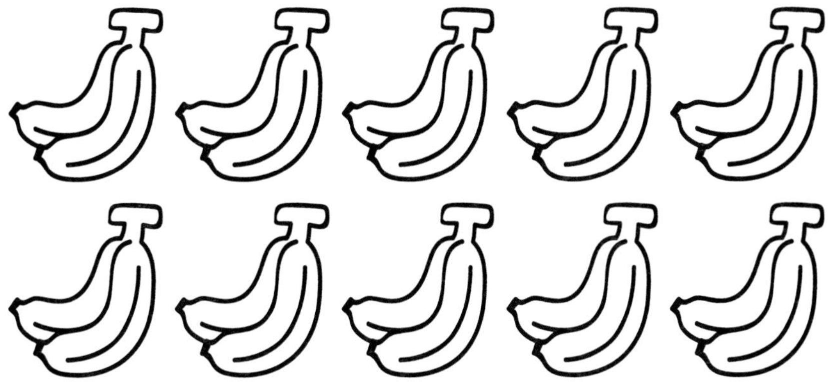

Twenty Bananas

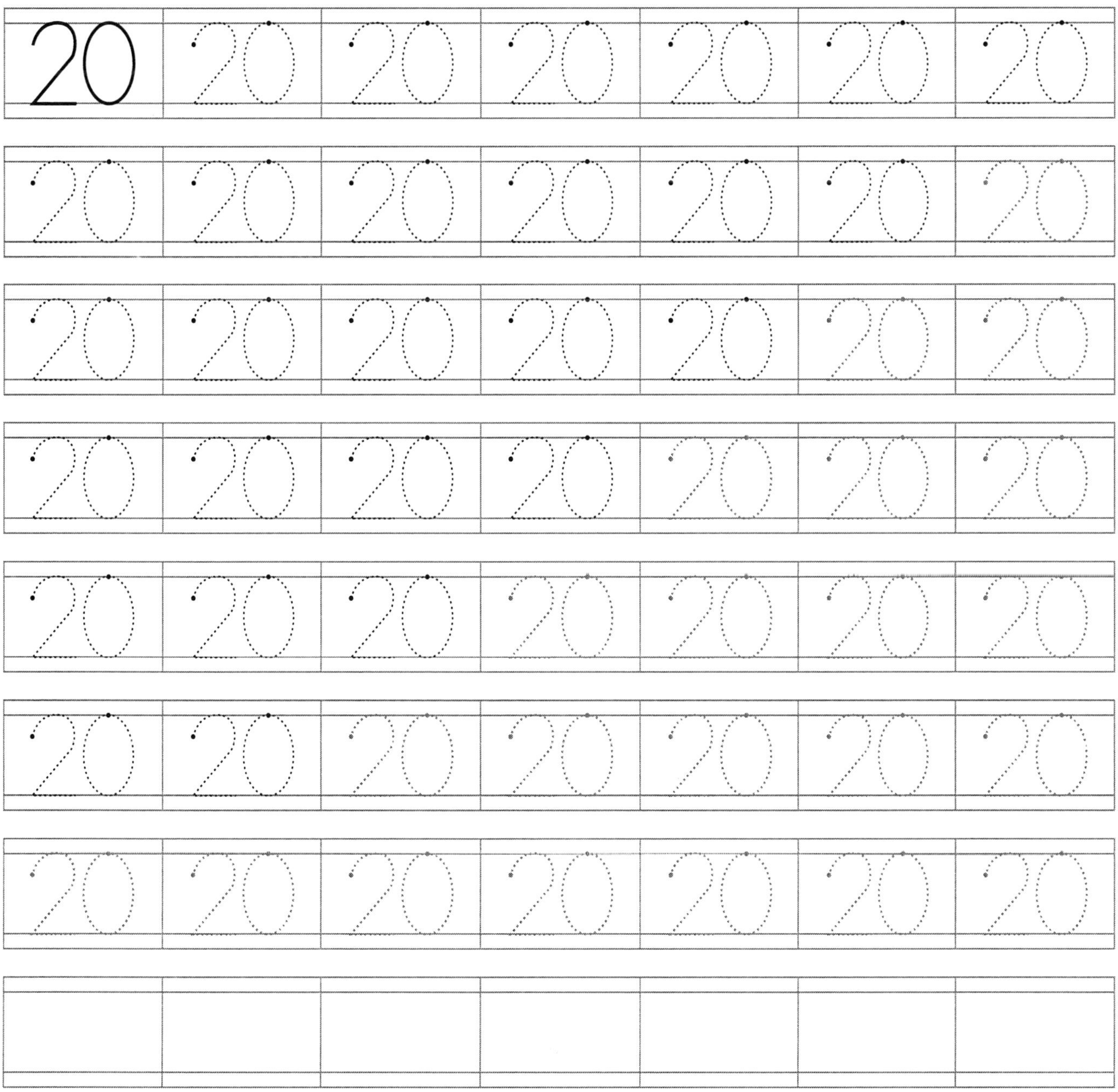

Say and trace numbers.

1	2	3	4
5	6	7	8
9	10	11	12
13	14	15	16
17	18	19	20

Write the numbers 1 to 20.

Date : .... Teacher's Signature : ....

Write missing numbers.

5		7		9
13				17
14	15		17	
7				11
16			19	20
1			4	
4	5			
10		12		
8			11	
11		13		

Date : ....

Teacher's Signature : ....

What comes before.

5	6			19			8			5
	10			12			16			9
	14			7			20			13
	3			2			11			17

What comes after.

1	2		10			3			5	
13			7			19			17	
6			18			8			16	
11			15			14			12	

What comes between.

1		3		2		4		15		17
5		7		6		8		4		6
11		13		10		12		7		9
17		19		16		18		13		15

Date : ....

Teacher's Signature : ....

Match the pictures with the numbers.

3

5

12

8

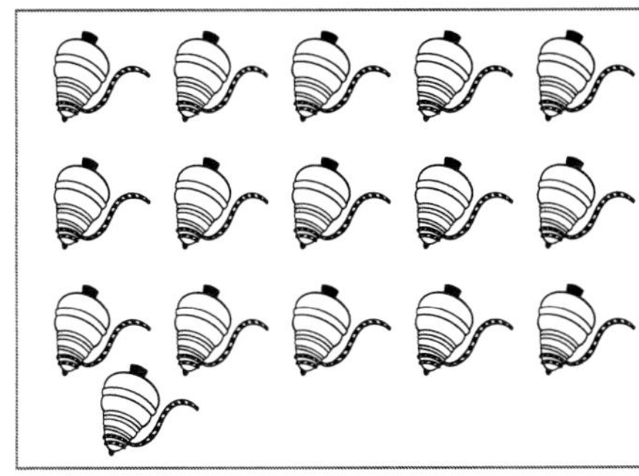

16

10

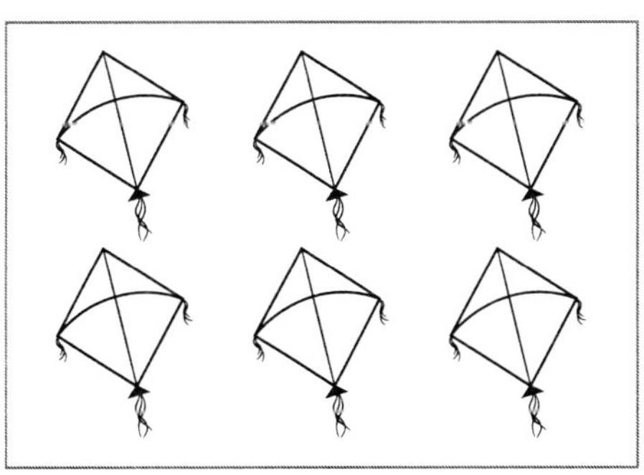

17

19

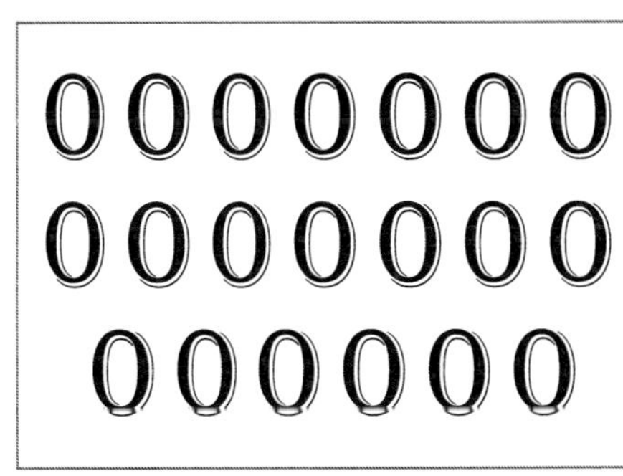

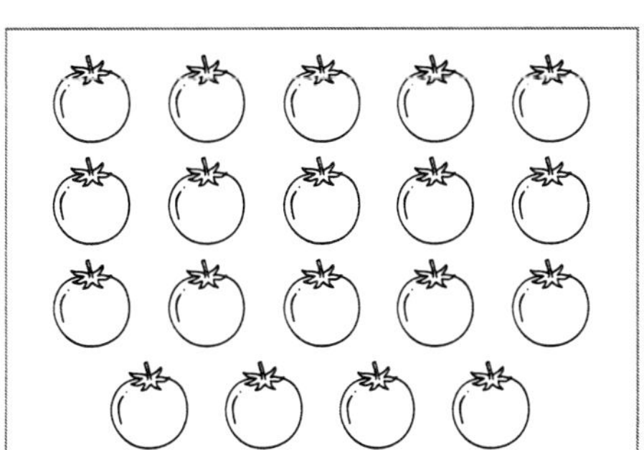

6

20

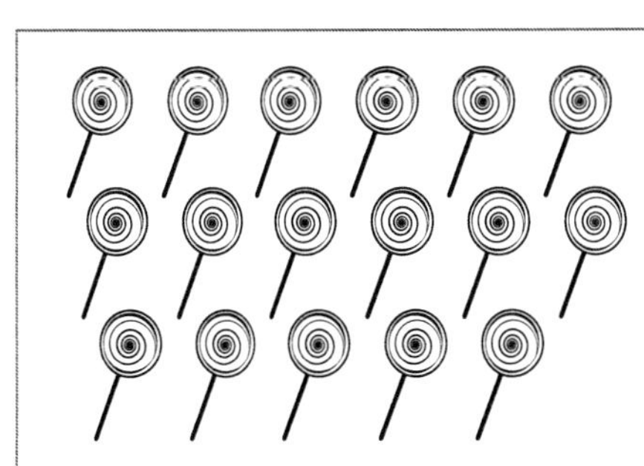

Date : ....

Teacher's Signature : ....

Count and encircle the correct number.

16

15

14

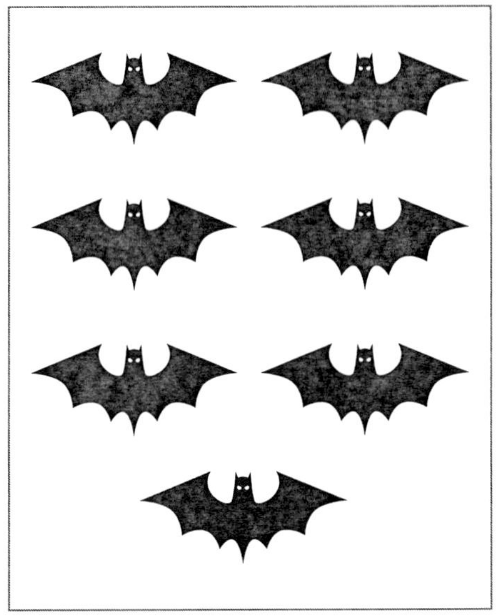

7

8

6

19

10

9

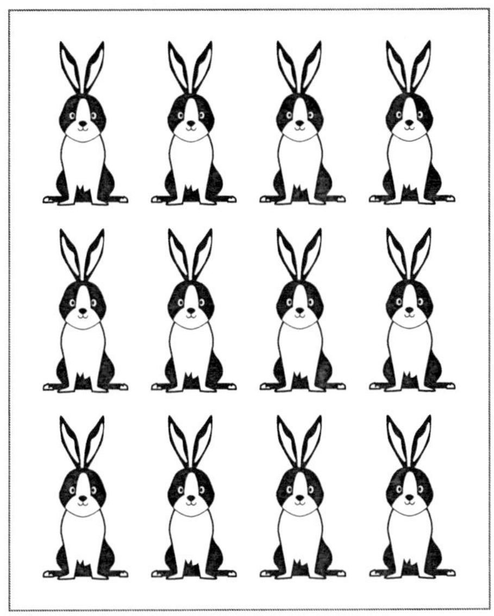

12

14

17

3

4

5

1

2

3

Date : ....

Teacher's Signature : ....

Write missing numbers.

8	2	9	4	14	11	20	19	13
10	9	8	1	10	20	4	8	11
12	20	2	11	7	17	12	16	2
9	16	8	9	18	12	16	10	12

Encircle the smaller number.

11	13	9	11	2	10	10	18	19
20	17	15	4	2	5	17	14	4
9	17	18	10	11	20	14	3	16
13	20	10	11	2	9	16	20	9

Date : ....

Teacher's Signature : ....

Write the numbers in increasing order.

1				
				20

Write the numbers in decreasing order.

20				
				1